The Wild Moonlight

LINDA BLACKMOOR

ISBN: 978-1-966417-08-8 (PRINT)

PUBLISHED BY QUILL PRESS. LINDA BLACKMOOR'S TITLES MAY BE PURCHASED IN BULK FOR EDUCATIONAL, BUSINESS, FUNDRAISING, OR SALES PROMOTIONAL USE. FOR INFORMATION, PLEASE EMAIL HELLO@LINDABLACKMOOR.COM

FIRST PRINT EDITION: 2024

LINDA BLACKMOOR
WWW.LINDABLACKMOOR.COM

Under the glow of the wild moonlight...

The opossum shuffles through damp leaves in search of insects and fruit.

Its pink, grasping tail helps it balance on mossy logs and fallen branches.

Within a soft belly pouch, tiny babies ride snug and hidden from view.

Quietly, it hunts the forest floor, making use of what others leave behind.

As North America's only marsupial, it finds adventure while the forest dreams.

Under the glow of the wild moonlight...

The fox steps lightly through fern-shadows and tangled roots.
Its tall, pointed ears listen closely for the soft movements of hidden prey.
A thick, russet tail provides warmth against the chill of long, quiet nights.
Omnivorous and resourceful, it samples mice, berries, and insects along its path.
From dense forests to open fields, the fox adapts steadily to each changing world.

Under the glow of the wild moonlight...

The Luna Moth unfolds from its silk-wrapped cocoon.

Feathery antennae sense subtle whispers carried on a gentle breeze.

Pale green wings, each with delicate tails, confuse hungry night birds.

Without a mouth, it does not feed—its short life devoted to finding a mate.

For but a few nights, it drifts beneath starlit leaves, an emblem of nature's fragile beauty.

Under the glow of the wild moonlight. . .

The skunk wanders quietly among mossy logs and damp leaves.

Its bold black-and-white stripes serve as a silent warning to hungry predators.

A keen nose and sturdy claws uncover grubs, seeds, and fallen fruit hidden in darkness.

When threatened, a spray of musk defends its peaceful search for a meal.

By night's end, this gentle scavenger helps keep the forest floor balanced and alive.

Under the glow of the wild moonlight. . .

The bobcat stalks quietly through leafy shadows.

Tufted ears and keen eyes track the rustle of mice and rabbits below.

A short, bobbed tail and dappled coat blend seamlessly with forest patterns.

By preying on the weak and unwary, it helps maintain nature's careful balance.

As dawn nears, it slips back into hidden dens, a silent guardian of the woodlands.

Under the glow of the wild moonlight...

The raccoon slips between broad oak trunks and feathery ferns.
Dexterous paws sift through streams and fallen logs for grubs and crayfish.
A masked face and ringed tail blend into the gentle hush of dusk.
The clever omnivore dines on berries, insects, and anything nature leaves behind.
With the first pale light of morning, it curls into its hollow, safe and still.

Under the glow of the wild moonlight...

The owl perches high above tangled roots and sleeping ferns.
Its eyes, shaped for darkness, find shapes where others see only shadow.
Asymmetrical ears guide its silent swoops toward a distant, scurrying sound.
Soft, fringed feathers hush its wings, letting it drift unseen between branches.
Before daylight stirs, it leaves small, tidy pellets—traces of its nightly feasts.

Under the glow of the wild moonlight...

The coyote patrols old trails woven through oak and pine.

Its howls and yips carry messages of shifting borders and neighboring kin.

In hidden dens, loving pairs nurture pups, teaching them subtle forest codes.

Able to flourish in deserts, suburbs, and woodlands, it embodies quiet resilience.

As dawn edges in, footprints vanish into brush and hollow dens.

Under the glow of the wild moonlight...

The brown bat darts through warm, humid air.

Echolocation guides its swift, silent turns, reading each insect's distant flutter.

By day, it clings inside hollow trees or attic rafters, wings folded in close repose.

In a single summer evening, it may devour hundreds of mosquitoes.

As autumn's chill approaches, it seeks dim caves to sleep through winter's freeze.

Under the glow of the wild moonlight...

The forest mice weave between fallen leaves, marking subtle trails.

Their sensitive whiskers guide them toward hidden seeds and tender shoots.

Nimble paws gather fallen seeds, some tucked away for winter, others forgotten.

In snug underground burrows, they nurture swift-growing families beneath the soil.

With short lifespans, often two years or less, they find purpose in growing their lineage.

Under the glow of the wild moonlight. . .

The armadillo roots gently through soft soil with its keen nose in search of grub.

Leathery armor shields it from hidden teeth and claws beneath low brush.

A rare feat among mammals, armadillos often birth identical quadruplets.

They cross small streams with ease, their inflated stomachs keeping them buoyant.

Limited sight yields to a powerful sense of smell, guiding it through the night.

Under the glow of the wild moonlight. . .

Fireflies shine their haunting lanterns across wildflower-carpeted meadows.
Tiny sparks, fueled by luciferin and oxygen, signal to waiting mates.
Each species follows a coded rhythm of evening light, unseen by day.
In their larval stage, they help control garden pests, balancing small ecosystems.
As warm nights unfold, these gentle flashes become a symphony of light.

Under the glow of the wild moonlight. . .

The hedgehog rustles through leaf litter in quiet, patient search.

Its short spines form a gentle shield, lifting against sudden threats.

Relying on a sharp nose, it finds juicy caterpillars, beetles, and slugs.

Resistant to certain snake venoms, some hedgehogs can dine on slithering serpents.

When winter's chill descends, it slows into hibernation beneath warm woodland soil.

www.ingramcontent.com/pod-product-compliance
Lightning Source LLC
Chambersburg PA
CBHW060838270326
41933CB00002B/127